BROTHERS

Brothers
© 2026 by E Gene Givens

The author guarantees that all content within this book is original and does not infringe upon the legal rights of any other individual or entity. The views expressed in this book are those of the author and do not necessarily reflect those of the publisher.

Printed originally in the United States of America

ISBN:
Paperback: 978-1-972299-51-7
Hardback: 978-1-972299-52-4
eBook: 978-1-972299-50-0

BROTHERS

E. Gene Givens

DEDICATION

we go to great lengths
and travel far
to pay a debt
or give recognition/tribute to
a man that's rich
long before
we would pay that same
debt to a man that's poor
and he could be
right outside your door
but we still do it
even though we know
that the rich are unworthy
and the poor need it more

CONTENTS

I USED TO SAY . . .

i used to say . . .
"i work two jobs!"
you know what i mean?
work *"two"* jobs!
didn't like working two jobs
but i liked saying
"i work two jobs!"

LINES . . .

lady said
stand
in that line
over there
i looked around
there were lines
everywhere

"Lines;" "Live Writers! Local On Tap," Page 24, Vol 1, Number 1, La Reina Press, Inc., Cincinnati, OH, 1979; and in "Lucidity," Second Quarter, 1991, Bear House Publishing, Houston, TX.

THREE PIECE SUIT AND UNEMPLOYED

it's a shock
me
articulate, attractive, well educated
and so distinctively unemployed
standing here with these
indignant, degenerate, social parasites
here in this long, long line . . .
legs sure are getting tired . . .
feet hurt so bad . . .
knees feel like they're about to lock . . .
if i'm not careful
i just might faint . . .
. . . but if i do that
i might lose my place in line

"Three Piece Suit and Unemployed," Live Writers! Local On Tap,
Page 24, Vol 1, Number 1, 1979, La Reina Press, Inc., Cincinnati, OH.

ON BEING COOL

i find it quite difficult
to be cool and collected
when i'm sweating
like a
buffalo
in a cashmere overcoat

POOL OF BETHESDA

(Serpentine Wall – Cincinnati)

they come
from penthouses, street corners
sweaty apartments and expensive chateaus
from asphalt ghettos and shopping center suburbs
faces without anonymity
punks, pimps, pushers, and ladies of the night
all working overtime
winos, shopping bag-ladies
the rich, the poor
the young and the old
by the droves they come
with picnic baskets, fried chicken, and barbecue
and with them, the ants and flies come too
streams of fatherless babies come
women with heavy backs and bent knees come
each, hoping to hear the secrets of life
empty faces
gazing at their reflections, and dreaming dreams
pitching pennies
pebbles
then watching the ripples disappear
they all come to the water for relief
and they all wait . . . and wait . . . and wait . . .
for a breeze . . .
for a breeze that would save

John 5:1-25: An angel of the lord went down at certain seasons into the pool and troubled the water; whoever stepped in first, after the troubling of the water, was healed of whatever disease he had.

AND THEY GATHERED

at first it was *"us"*
then there was as many of *"them"*
as there were of *"those"*
the group that seemed to be
"hanging around"
began to dissipate
but the odd assortment gathered there
remained the same – short ones, tall ones
fat/obese ones, little ones, young, and old ones
when one was helped
there was another to take that space
there was a couple of old ones
creeping up and down the aisles
like they were in some type of blind trance
one of the fat ones
hopelessly struggled to get out of a chair
while another struggled to get into one
a few secretly sipped on their liquid lunch
of muscatel or md 20-20
some smoked
defiling the no smoking signs
some were very familiar with the routine
and took a short snooze
knowing it would be a while
and they wouldn't miss any news
i guess they all kept asking themselves
"why?" . . .
"why am i doing this?"
and their empty pockets
and their empty contracting stomachs replied
"why not?"

"And They Gathered...," "Athenaeum," Page 22, Volume, LXIV, Number 1, Winter 1979, Xavier University, Cincinnati, OH; and in "Pierian Spring," October 1991, Mile High Poetry Society, Denver, CO.

PIPE DREAMS

i had a dream
of someone or something that i wanted to be
a dream so clear, that its end i could almost see
i wanted to be different, than all the rest
unique i would be, at my best
i would get an education
aspire to several degrees
with the most-highest
being a ph.d
i would be a *"professional"*
make great sums of money
buy that house that the average person could not afford
drive a car that hummed, instead of roared
give moms all the things she wished for
but never had
change her troubled look from sad to glad
i would put my niece through school
if it took the last dollar i had
i would have a butler, butcher, and a maid
and all my friends would say
i had it *"made in the shade"*
my reason for wanting all these things
had nothing to do with my happiness
my sanity, or me
i was the last of nine
and the first to get a degree
and i was living pieces of *"their"*
pipe dreams
that they had shoved on me

"Pipe Dreams," "Athenaeum," Page 18, Volume, LXIV, Number 2, Spring 1980,
Xavier University, Cincinnati, OH.

COMPLIMENTS

black as sin...black hearted...black as night...coon-ass darkie...
spear-chucking blackies . . . lazy schwartze . . . little brownie...
pickaninny...half-breed groid . . . crazy kaffir . . . jim
crow . . . lazy blue-gum . . . mayonnaise monkey...slit-slut
rastas . . . eye servants . . . low-down shine...grits & gravy
sambo . . . watermelon eating...triflin' spade...grimy toad...
jive-timin' "niglet"...belly crawlin' burr-head . . . sooty spook . . .
jigga-boo . . . i'm a little "tea-pot"...uncle tom. . . slow ass
jungle bunny. . . moon-cricket. . . balloon-lipped mulignan . . .
walk like a mouli . . . foolish nig-nog . . . tar-baby. . .you fight
like a munt . . . worm-faced mayate . . . bootlip macaco . . .
ebonics . . . thick-lip tobacco-brain nigger . . . bounty-bar
oreo . . . nothin' but gator-bait . . . crazy ass mau-mau . . . stupid
petrol sniffer . . . fat ass sheboon . . . porch-monkey . . . eight-
ball spook . . . dumb ass niggas

PERSEVERANCE

we are just tired of being tired . . .
tired of dealing with all this stuff
all by ourselves
it seems, the issues are not getting any smaller
only bigger and bigger

you think you solved one problem
and two more spring up in its place: segregation; war; racial
intolerance; wire taps; assassinations; interracial marriages;
church bombings; welfare; crime; racism; inadequate
education; illiteracy; lead paint; low birth weight; equal pay;
sexual preferences; racial profiling; unemployment; high blood
pressure; hiv; sickle cell; black lgbt rights; systemic racism;
teen pregnancy; starvation; diabetes; black killings; voting
rights; drugs; urban blight; unjust prison sentences; poverty,
etc., etc., etc.

we are just tired of being tired . . .
just so tired of dealing with all this stuff
all by ourselves
tell me america, is this justice?
or, is it just us?

when are you going to stop
standing on the side lines
waiting for the next new study
the next speech
or the next commission
and start involving yourselves
and start loving us back
and use some that white privilege
to give us some strength
so we can deal with all this sh**

LIKE WILD HORSES . . .

herded
like wild horses
and caged like wild animals
were our bodies
minds/souls/spirits . . .

tamed and trained
then released
to romp and run and feed
on fresh/familiar/new
grass . . .
insight . . .
knowledge . . .
truth . . .

herded and caged
tamed and trained
then released

each time
just long enough . . .

for some of us to . . . escape

THIS IS NOT AN OBSERVATION

our kings . . . our people . . . our spirits were kidnapped and bound with hemp and chains; their flesh sold like beasts of burden, and exiled to unknown lands, where their feet found no ground, the stars were unfamiliar, and freedom became just a dream

places where they with their heirs passed into the anonymity of slavery, and with them also passed our true history . . . our true heritage . . . our true legacy, and now we search blindly and become lost in legends handed down in mystical folk lore, only told in secret places by those poisoned by the fairy tale of the *"... and they lived happily ever after"*

we have no true reference point to start from. . . to go to; we have no stars . . . no maps to guide us; we cannot shoot an azimuth to our desired location; we have no magnetic north to keep us on track; no magic word that will open doors; no wise sage . . . no man who has made the journey . . . often enough, that he is now considered an *"expert"*

we know not our fathers, nor their fathers. their unwanted features, and unmarketable characteristics, have been all but eliminated . . . we now look/act strange . . . odd . . . different even to ourselves

some of us still cling desperately to vague hopes . . . dreams . . . memories; only notions of the past; while others grow senile in their youth, and never begin the search

it seems we have been intentionally deprived, coerced, and forced to learn the process. . . the process of assimilation, and in that process, we were consumed, incorporated, absorbed, and overcome by dis/association

(Continued)

we now act out, what we have been taught . . . told . . .
shown by others, except our own, what is appropriate . . .
courteous and polite. hypnotically, we lost the will to question . . .
to challenge . . . to fight for what was/is ours

we have been nurtured . . . grown . . . developed like vegetables in a garden into good and bad "niggas" and now . . . we must ask permission with acquiescent smiles and lowered eyes, or suffer the stigmas and labels of a society. . . a culture, of intolerance, greed, and duplicity

we have been conditioned, like Pavlov's dog, and we have learned well, how to obediently accept and endure our kings' portion of racism . . . self-hatred . . . ignorance . . . unemployment . . . drugs . . . profiling . . . and death

this phenomenon is not an observation, i did not have to live 400 years to feel, or see these things. no, i did not live 400 years. . . i am just one of many who became tired. . . and lost in their search for self-reliance . . . for the hidden treasure of self-esteem. . . for reference. . .

for familiarity . . . awareness. . . for power – the sixth
angel . . . for knowledge . . . comprehension . . . and for wisdom

i now wait for a word. . . an act. . . a sign. . . a sign that would reveal a great secret, a justifiable reason, a hidden truth. . . for something/anything real and true, that would lead me to the tombs of my fathers, and the true meaning of liberty, freedom, equality . . . and emancipation

UNTIL I AM NO LONGER A MAN

i am a man
so, i must not cry, you said
you told me, i was a man
and i must provide for my family
i must be reliable, dedicated, and brave
i must work hard, and be productive
even when no jobs are available
i am a man, you said
so, i must suffer all the verbal insults
and the systemic racism and discrimination
and all the other things
that keep me from doing all the things i must do
i am a man, you said
so, i must not show any sensitive emotions
and i must try to understand *"the way things are"*
i must . . . i must . . . i must
but i say
yes, i am a man
but first, i am me . . . a black man; and i will cry
when i feel pain; i will walk the thin line between cowardice
and bravery, and try to control the darkness, and the fear
that surrounds me everyday; i will love, and hope to be loved
by someone in return, regardless of their education, race, or
their financial situation; i will always show emotions that fit
the occasion because . . . i am a man
yes, i am a man
i will respect all that you have taught me, and i will try to use
things from your generation, but. . . i will not lose my self-
respect, and bow down to racist, and their sympathizers
and i will continue to ask the hard questions,
and weigh the answers, no matter who syes, stands before me
this i will do
until i am no longer a man

GLACIER HWY – MILE MARKER 42

(Juneau, Alaska)

to escape to a place
out of time
not knowing/caring
when the sun
rises/sets
where feeling/being relaxed are one
to have searched and found your
piece of the rock
and to sense/know/feel
the peace it brings
with the knowledge that
glacier hwy – mile marker 42
will be there tomorrow undaunted
by all who pass by

"Glacier Hwy – Mile Marker 42," "Select American Poetry," Page 22, Vol 1,
Phoenix Publications, Atlanta, GA.

GRAY EDGES

living on the gray edge
of ink-black nights
and paper-white days
i lose all sense of time/reality/me then i remember . . .
i am black
in a world where time seeks change
but can only find arrogant mediocrity
but when i dream
i dream in un-colors
where the nights are without time and going off the gray edge
makes equality become real

"Gray Edges," "Voices On the Wind," Vol II, Winter 1989, The Poet's Corner, Baltimore, MD.

THE VIEWING

(for Burdetta)

i don't need to see no body!
i don't care if it's a presumed ritual
that predates human history
i just want to remember them
just like i remember them
you know, just like they were
how they looked
how they laughed
how they smiled
all the things they said to me
and all the things
we said to each other
i don't mind covering the mirrors
and stopping the clocks from ticking
and throwing salt over my left shoulder
and giving the family my condolences
or providing support
and sharing the family's grief
but i just don't need to view
or see no shell of a dead body
not the body of the loving person
i want to remember
you can cremate them
or put them in, or above the ground
no matter . . .
i still don't need to see no dead body

EDWINA, AL, AND ME:
LIVE AT THE HOBBIT

you could say
we had church that night
people were clapping
shouting
and testifying out loud
compelled by fascination
and the syncopated rhythms
we lost control
i started poeting
Al started composing
and Edwina started hugging
and kissing
people she didn't even know
one by one
our hearts and pulses quickened
until we jumped up
and out
of our bodies
into an atmosphere
of musical bliss
like jubilant skydivers
leaping from an aircraft
in an organized freefall
with everyone pulling their parachute
at the same time
and catching their breath
just before hitting the ground
when it was over
we returned to our senses
and realized that we had been . . .
jazz-merized
by the reverend mel brown's jazz quintet

NUBIAN REFUGE

oh, nubian queen
adorned in gold, silk, and black lace oh, queen-mother of
nations come nurture me, and renew my warrior spirit come
weave your exotic spell upon my soul speak to me with your
subtle touch say to me with your unveiled eyes

> *"come, my son . . .*
> *come rest your head upon my bosom*
> *and let me run my fingers through your hair let*
> *me massage your troubled brow come . . .*
>
> *come rest and dream your forgotten dreams . . .*
> *dreams of innocence, equality, peace, and love come*
> *let me fold you in my arms so i can share your pain*
> *and breathe new life into you*
> *come let me prepare and strengthen you for the many*
> *challenges you must face the sun will rise anew on*
> *tomorrow*
> *and i will make you strong . . . once more . . .*
> *for the new journey that is about to unfold"*

TOMORROW...

we were born with a death sentence on our heads; not like capone, jesse james, john dillinger, or pretty boy floyd; bonified criminals who committed numerous crimes.
my birth made me worse than a criminal; something less than human; a subject to be ruled over; someone who needed overseeing, like the slaves of yesteryear, using their ropes, chains, neck restraints, and dogs. or, just like on any other yesterday . . . like on monday, tuesday, wednesday, thursday, friday, saturday, and don't forget sunday; the day of rest. for whom? not us! all i see are brothers and sisters being verbally abused, harassed, intimidated, assaulted, and murdered every day. . . just because. . .

we go to early church service, and then we still must get out there and hustle for that low, or minimum wage service and hospitality jobs that still requires an overseer to supervise, just to make sure we are dressed smartly in the company's uniform, smiling and grinning, and obediently doing what we are told

no matter what we do to conform and assimilate, our color, our features, give us away, and they all know that we have been labeled as *"less than."* even the privileged few are shocked when they are treated like the rest of us – insignificant, and void of human rights and justice; always sticking a microphone, or the barrel of a gun in our faces when something goes down. they are shocked when they become one of the yellow, red, black, and brown groups that need to be put in their place - the place of subjugation when they get caught abusing their authorization to rule, they get scared, and run to the microphones, and act like the puppets that they are, and tell us how they are one of us, and how thorough they will be in their defense, or how thorough they will be in in their investigation for justice;   the justice they will soon   see, will   take forever before anything is seen, or done. Just like that Breonna Taylor kind of justice

how thorough is justice, anyway? everyone knows, no matter the color, that the riots during the watts rebellion, and the protests and marches in ferguson, st. louis, minneapolis, portland, mississippi, alabama, or new york, were caused by a lack of that so-called "thorough justice." justice came quickly in some places, so did the changes of the laws that impacted the community. is this what must be done to get your attention – marches, protests, and riots?

what we fail to understand is that the people . . . the people of privilege, ideal of justice comes from a different place – a different perspective – a different world, where the system is "really" blind. . . blind to us. . . it is a place where the rivers of justice flow abundantly without obstruction 'cause, when you make the rules, you can make sure that the rules are not applicable to anyone with my face; my race; or anyone suffering with my case in the end, we still be a people from the projects and ghettos, still searching, still waiting, for Sherman's Field Order #15 that gave us 40 acres and a mule; hoping that something, somewhere, would yield a piece of land that we thought we could call *"my place;"* a place where we could define what justice was/is; but Johnson rescinded the order, and took our dream away, and gave the 40 acres, and that mule back to the confederate slavers. is that thorough justice?

how many centuries must we wait for the reparations of justice? this situation is beyond a dream deferred. they shot the Kennedys, Martin, and Malcom too, as well as anyone else of color that stood up for change and justice.

instead of wearing hoods, and burning crosses, they started hunting us in blue and white collars, controlling the schools, factories, colleges, and un/professional jobs; then city councils, the chief of police, mayors, governors, secretary of state, state and senate representatives in the state houses, and in the congress and the senate

instead of wearing hoods, and burning crosses, they started hunting us in blue and white collars, controlling the schools, factories, colleges, and un/professional jobs; then city councils, the chief of police, mayors, governors, secretary of state, state and senate representatives in state house, and in the congress and the senate; places where they could control us with laws, that could stop progress and justice; racial profiling, no knock warrants, batons, hoods, neck restraints, zip-ties, tasers, rubber bullets, and tear gas. so now, they are after our vote; closing polling places, destroying mail boxes, removing us from the voting roles, and paying for intimidating messages on our tv's to promote doubt and fear they have stabbed section 5 of Representative John R. Lewis' 1965 voting rights act right in the heart. he has passed on, and now, they want to honor him at the Alabama state house, Atlanta, and the capitol rotunda, with thousands of dollars in flowers. if they really wanted to honor him, they could pass the new voting rights bill.

but, it seems like it's that same ole, same ole line - just be patient, we need to conduct a study to see what's right; we need you to just wait, be patient, and you will get the justice that you are entitle to; just wait, we need to appoint a commission to look at things; we need to appoint a grand jury to conduct a thorough investigation; just be polite, and wait your turn; we will get to you soon . . . just wait; just wait, we'll make sure that you will get justice; you know, it's a structural racial problem, that will take time to fix . . . so, you just have to wait . . . until tomorrow.

but, John R. Lewis would say that you should not wait until tomorrow to to march; he would remind you, to not wait . . . he would say *"if not now, then when?"* he would say that you should go speak truth to power; that you should not wait to protest; to get up from watching everything happening to you on your TV screen, or on your IPhones; to go get into some good trouble, and don't wait until tomorrow . . . to make your own revolution go speak truth to power; that you should not wait to protest; to get up from watching everything happening to you on your TV screen, or on your IPhones; to go get into some good trouble, and don't wait until tomorrow . . . to make your own revolution today!

WE HOLD THESE TRUTHS . . .

we hold these truths
to be self-evident
that only white people
think they deserve freedom and justice
as if they are entitled to give it
or take it, at will
and award it to whomever
they may choose

however . . .
freedom is the power . . .
a right to act, speak
or think, as one wants
without hindrance or restraint
and choice is an act
of selecting or deciding
when faced with two or more
people, places, or things

in the end,

freedom is simply a state

of not being imprisoned or enslaved
exercising the natural rights of freedom
to go or stay
to move, or not to move
to speak, or not to speak
and no man has the right
or power
to consider both
'cause true freedom is . . .
what it is . . .
freedom

LIVE AT THE HOBBIT

(Portland Oregon)

we hung out
in middle-earth
at the hobbit – in portland
listening to some jazz
and hoping to see
what we could see
which turned out to be
nothing
but our sensory fibers
had an auditory feast
as five brothers
carved up the air
like trolls
looking for the magic ring

JAZZ-MERIZED

my skin just slid off
i couldn't even stop it
i just sat there
hypnotized
glassy-eyed
and bare to the bone
as they played
i listened
helpless
and unknowing
all i could do was smile
shake my head
from side to side
and pat my feet
to the down beat

"Jazz-merized," "Wide Open Magazine," Summer 1991, Wide Open Magazine, Santa Rosa, CA.

LEANING ON AIR

the bar room in panama
was a smoky mix of rum
cigarettes, and reefer fumes

the juke box was on blast
drowning out the shots outside
and the dance floor
was hot and crowded
with brothers and sisters
in the zone
gracefully leaning on air

the tables that laced the room
were occupied
with brothers and sisters
"rapping for the go home"
while in the other room
jubilant souls
were still on the floor
dancing on air to the madison
echoing *"oh yeah!"*
and *"party over here!"*

the place was lit
waiting
for last call
and the lights to come on
so they could
adjust themselves to reality and
their feet
could gracefully
touch the ground . . .
once again

WHEN I GROW UP . . .

(For Mitchell, Vernon, Vicky, Tony, and Lee)

when i grow up, there's going to be a radical
or sweeping change
or maybe even a clean sweep.

i might just get international, and be a coup d'état
and generate an uprising or even a rebellion.

i might just get low-down and break up, upset
or overthrow somebody.

maybe i'll cause a reversal, a debacle, a cataclysm
or even a convulsion.

if i ain't careful, i might even be a rotating, turning gyration or
a spinning, revolving cycle.

i mean, i might even change things – radically
and rebel, remodel, recast, and/or reform the situation.

i might get artistic and simply change the face of something or,
i might get real-real
and just break with the traditional past.

i mean, i might revolve, rotate, turn, spin, gyrate
whirl and twirl, if i ain't careful.

i might even get domestic and be a rebellious insurgent

a radical reversionist, or even a cataclysmic partisan.

or, maybe i might just settle on being me,
and be my own hero
and if that's the case,
there's definitely going to be a revolution . . .
or anything else i want to be.

25

WAITING ON THE LORD

"you're not alone," you said
to *"turn the other cheek"*
when they tormented and mistreated me
and place me beneath their feet
so, with tear stained face, i stood and waited
quiet, humble, and meek
i just wanted my own space
some peace
to be left alone
and a home that i could call *"my place"*
instead
i got a whip on my back
a cotton sack
and a small, one room shack
since then
i've been the last hired
first fired
and my spirit is sure getting tired
Lord
as God is my judge
you know i don't like to hold a grudge
but Lord
i only got two cheeks,
one back,
and two feet
and opportunities and jobs
ain't getting no better
and now
they seem to be killing us off
one by one
at least
two or three of us
every week

BROTHERS – PART I

(for those of you that don't understand)

"brothers" are just like any other brothers, what makes them unique is that they are *"my"* brothers; they may be your father, uncle, brother, son, cousin, nephew, or best friend on the stoop, or on the corner; they may be a fellow member, a fellow country man, or just a fellow man; my brothers treat everyone with respect, until you give them a reason not to; they know that giving respect and agreement are not the same, so, you should be careful, because they have grown strong on grits, chicken giblets, rice, black eyed peas, collar greens, and pot liquor, and for sure, they do not suffer chicken shits' and fools

have you not seen the unmatched intestinal fortitude of my brothers? have you not recognized their courage and stamina? have you not observed the bravery, valor, and endurance, and their willingness to face, or to confront, the agony and pain? have you not seen the danger that the system continues to inflict upon them, and their willingness to face uncertainty, or, the intimidation that stands before them each day in blue; they have faced so many painful challenges in their lives, without blinking an eye, though you remain silent, i am sure that this has not gone unnoticed

you may know about the physical courage of many of my brothers; their bravery has caused them to stand in the face of physical pain, hardships, threats of death, and even death, itself; but what i most admire is my brother's moral courage; their ability to act rightly, despite the risk of adverse consequences and in the face of criticism, shame, and popular opposition. i mean, their ability to do the right thing is unquestioned, and is deserving of ribbons and medals

Brothers – Part I

(Continued)

so, do not take my brothers and the brotherhood for granted, for when my brothers bleed, we all bleed; when they die, a piece of all the brethren die; when they cringe, when they get bludgeoned with billy-clubs and pipes by soldiers, and choke holds by the boys in blue, with pain and disgust, we cringe too; and as day turns to night, rubber bullets, and chemical and pepper pellets fly, always looking for the right spot.

BROTHERS – PART II

then, pepper spray, and tear gas comes to disrupt, and blind our eyes. ironically, rubber bullets, pepper pellets, tear gas, and pepper spray, these contraptions are things are used to protect some people from wild animals.

the system thinks that we brothers are supposed to respect their systematic violence, belittling words, and racial slurs, choke holds, neck restraints, police tasers, and undisciplined words, just trying to control us. . . with free, home-made lobotomy's, or, to just kill us

all that shit makes you want to. . . makes you feel like you have to . . . have to run and escape, and run, run, and run some more, just to hide, like running from a lion, or a rabid dog; some run, playing the long game, to come back on another day; some march, to hide, because there is safety in numbers; some go to work, to hide some more; some do nothing, and hide anyway; some hide behind other brothers, in an attempt to escape; some brothers escape, and hide, and take to the nod; some pimp, and some go lean on chemicals to get by; some religions devote themselves to the brothers; some brothers devote themselves to the religion; others become a religion all by them selves; still, others take from the offering plate; while some brothers fight for justice; some brothers fight for just us; while some still just keep running, trying to escape

other brothers turn their rifles on their own, while hiding behind the night, or a badge, but the moon, and the skin don't lie; in the real, you just be a brother, a fellow member of the fraternity, a fellow country man, or just a brother who is a fellow man, like all the other brothers who run to escape the system and their home-made psychosurgery that tries to confuse us into losing our self-will, our spontaneity, our

(Continued)

responsiveness, our self-awareness, our responsibility, and our self-control

so, for those of you that don't understand. . . you see, "brothers" are just like any other brothers. what makes them unique is that they are "my" brothers who are your fathers, uncles, brothers, sons, cousins, nephews and best friends, out there challenging, protesting, marching, and in the big houses, fighting for your rights, trying to make a difference, and achieving a righteous change for you and your children

A PICTURE ROCKWELL NEVER PAINTED

(a poem for Ricky Rouse)

motionless
he watches . . .
a piece of sun light
sifting through the window
of sandwich sized bars
that make checkerboard shadows
across his body
as wind-blown scents
permeate his senses
and disturbs old spider webs
and stagnant dust particles
that occupy his cell. . . his soul
his only thought. . .
"i wonder why Norman Rockwell never painted . . .
this part of America?"

*"A Picture Rockwell Never Painted," "Windows On The World," Vol 2, Summer 1991of Poetry,
The National Library, Owings, MD,*

A FORMULA FOR CHANGE

politicians react to the media
and the media to drama
if i . . . you. . . me. . . we
make the drama
the media will come
and the politicians
will respond
and
change
will occur
because
a conscientious politician
doesn't want to
"look bad"
. . . especially on CNN and MSNBC

NIGRITUDE

(for Jerome)

i be
you be
he/she/it be
we be a people
locked
in a land of
time sequence
"to be"
forever
i be wantin'
you be doin'
he/she/it be goin'
to some magical destination
in time
i be
you be
he/she/it be
from generation to generation
we be a people
fruitlessly searching for the keys
that will open the doors to the world of
i am . . . you are . . . he/she/it is . . .
some people call it illiteracy
incorrect grammar
but it's not
its **black** english
and it just
be. . .

"N I g r I t u d e"

THE SUPERVISOR

my supervisor - a white man, told me to my face, that he liked my kind; and that he couldn't understand why i was caught up with these issues concerning the whole black race; how we got on the subject, i don't recall, but it was strange how he considered his opinion as special, good, noble, and obviously the best for all

he started off saying, color'ds didn't need a voting rights bill; he said he just couldn't understand how, or why, the color'ds could vote for Obama, or black women, or even Joe, and not a good white man; that the color'ds should vote for someone who would make america great again; that he saw no reason for the color'ds to support the causes of MLK, Chisholm, Jackson, Vivian, Lewis, or BLM; that they all had major character flaws; and it was stupid to make MLK's birthday a holiday, after all; that there were better people who had done more for the color'd race; that welfare made them color'ds lazy and mean, and it taught them how to exploit the system, and not look for work, it seemed

silent, i remained, as he tried to get me to enlist into his diatribe; then he said that color'ds were ungrateful, after all the things that whites had done for them; that he doubted if systemic racism really happened to anyone; that discrimination was a myth, and since it never happened to him, it really didn't exist; that the color'ds were just using it as an excuse for their lack of qualifications, and family abuse

you should have seen his raspberry face, when i told him the news about my race; things got so quiet, you could hear a pin drop in the place; i began to laugh so hard until tears ran down my face, 'cause my supervisor - the white man, thought i was a foreigner, or of hispanic descent, and he did not realize how a black man could be quiet, and politely listen to all of his sh**

KOREA:
LAND OF THE MORNING CALM

he has come to a land
where the morning is calm
and the mist clings to the mountains
as dew to the leaves

he was equal here – even superior
and they were the outcasts

    (in their own land)

he marvels at their efficiency... their ingenuity...
their never-ending struggle with poverty
and their ideal of unification

in this land, nimble fingers fabricate the unexpected
some sow seeds in barren land

    (they feed the multitudes)

others arm themselves with plastic smiles ...
and sad faces
still others, use their bodies in trade

their pain cannot be seen – only imagined
as they rise, faithfully, with the early morning mist
to meet the twentieth-first century

they are a simple people, embedded in tradition
they are a wise and shrewd people
a nation who has mastered the art . . . the technique
of making you feel . . . believe that you are important
while they empty your pockets

. . . but this is as it should be
for a visitor – a stranger of color
in a land where the morning is calm
and the mist clings to the mountains
as dew to the leaves

TEN CLICKS FROM THE DMZ

(Camp Edwards, Korea)

there must have been birds there . . .
but at this moment
he could not remember seeing one

he remembered the ambush patrols . . . the bone chilling
winter . . . the dead batteries . . . and the smoke . . . the smoke
that percolated from those little farm shacks; he remembered
the sudden rain . . . the humidity . . . and the floods that
followed

he remembered the heat . . . in May . . . June . . . July . . . and in
August; he remembered how he often tried to stand motionless
hoping to escape, but the perspiration leaked from his pours
anyway

he remembered the landscape . . . the people . . . their
customs: the three-man shovel . . . the rice fields carved into
the side of the mountains . . . the home-made rice wine, and
the kimchi carts that doubled as the family station wagon and
pick-up truck

he remembered the emerald green rice fields in spring, and
how, just before harvest, they looked like a sea of shimmering
gold, as they danced and waved in the currents of a smooth
summer wind

he remembered how they celebrated holidays . . . the
young . . . the old . . . and the dead; and he remembered that
dog . . . that dog that he thought was the unit's mascot . . .
that dog that he encouraged everyone to feed – to give their
food scraps to . . . that same dog that had grown to be so
beautiful . . . that dog that he saw hanging from the bridge
– struggling and gasping for air . . . that same dog that turned
out to be someone's holiday dinner . . . then he
remembered . . . he didn't like celebrating holidays after that

from time to time, he can remember many things about being there, but it's strange that he couldn't seem to remember seeing any birds there, or find the words to appropriately describe the smell . . . that smell that burned your nostrils, and made your eyes start to water . . . that piercing smell. . . that he will never forget that gut-wrenching smell . . . of life . . . and death . . .
10 clicks from the dmz

COLORS

in a city/place
surrounded by mountains
of water/clouds/stone
and people
there can be no escape
(if there is such a thing)
to move through
time and space
is to move into
a domain where
one
is always a dominant force
so, relax
and enjoy the colors
of blue/green oceans
grey/blue/black clouds
of mountains and people
that change colors
where ever you go

THOUGHTS CONCERNING I . . .

"Answers To Test"

You can give people the answers to the test, but their lack of confidence, self esteem, or will power makes them easily influenced by outside or other unknown spiritual forces. Consequently, they will ignore the "right" answer and end up flunking the test, anyway.

"Control"

In organizations, there are three main types of internal controls: detective, preventive, and corrective. controls are typically policies and procedures, or technical safeguards that are implemented to prevent problems and protect the assets of the organization. people need to develop internal controls to identify or prevent, unhealthy behavior. in relationships, there are indicators of unhealthy behavior like: the pressure of commitment; unrealistic expectations; isolation; blaming; hypersensitivity; threats and coercion; battering; and other similar unhealthy behaviors. some people do all they can to deny their feelings, hiding behind a façade of control. they fail to show their vulnerabilities, passions, and true feelings. they make the other person jump through hoops trying to prove their love, or demand perfection in how they dress, how they talk, etc., or, want future reassurances, that they will never really be satisfied with. the only way to deal with this type of person is to check with your internal controls and remove yourself – as early as possible.

"Guarantees"

No one wants to take any kind of risk; everyone seems to want guarantees from the other person before they even consider taking a risk.

The "Real" One/Thing"

From my experience, people don't know how to recognize the "real" one/thing. Or they fail to recognize the real one/thing only **after it's gone.**

THOUGHTS CONCERNING II . . .

"Bad Habits"

Bad habits are nonproductive. Habits like lying, smoking, cheating, stealing, duplicity, and acts against the law, anything socially unacceptable will do. However, the risk, the adventure, is so exciting that we go to great lengths to adopt one, or many of them. Some people are totally encompassed by bad habits; striving to find one that fits their unique personality. One that is similar to everyone else, hoping that they can hide themselves among the masses, or just pretend that they don't exist, until they are suddenly found out. Then they start blaming it on some associate: "He introduced to me . . ." "He made me . . ." "She left the money out in the open . . ." "It's all your fault!"

"Game of Life"

Many people like to stand on the sidelines and second-guess other people's situations, actions, motives, intentions, and feelings. But from my experience, there is nothing like being "in the game." The rush and exhilaration you experience at the beginning. The heart pounding excitement of anticipating the other person's next move. The intensity, the passion, the pain, and the joy that comes at the end. Simply stated: the "game" is just like the lottery commercial says, "You will never have a chance to win, if you don't buy a ticket to play."

THOUGHTS CONCERNING III . . .

"Fear to Succeed"

Life has dealt you the cards you have played – you didn't ask for them. In playing the hand you was dealt, some hands you have won, some hands you have lost. Many people comment on how they would not have gone through the things that you have experienced. That's because they are only focusing on the negative or unsuccessful outcomes. They failed to see/hear the positive, because of their own fear of failure.

Sometimes I wonder if it's really their fear to succeed that drives them, and not their fear of failure. Because when you fail you can quit, make excuses, and issue blame – that's the easy out! When you succeed you have to constantly take risks and fail. The more failures you experience . . . the more lessons you learn . . . the wiser you become. You learn to recognize failure before it occurs. Success is no secret – that's the easy part. Once you have worked at achieving success, people forget that you also have to try to maintain it – and that's the hard part!

My observations have revealed that people get involved with one another and have expectations that are deserving, but very unrealistic. Often, they fail to considered that the other person (or themselves) may not have the skill, ability, attitude, aptitude, inclination, or motivation to achieve and maintain in business, relationships, love, marriage, trust, happiness, dependability, passion, stability, security, etc. There can be many reasons why they don't possess the necessary characteristics. They can range from lack of experience, maturity, knowledge, desire, etc., you name it. As a result, they spend their time hiding the truth from themselves and others; constantly making excuses for themselves, as well as the other person, for their unsuccessful endeavors. As a result their energies are spent maneuvering in, around, and through situations/people, in an attempt to keep their shortcomings undiscovered. They are too busy hiding that they don't have the time to focus on overcoming shortcomings, or preparing themselves for real success.

INHERITANCE

she felt uncomfortable
because there was no object
to serve as a bridge between father and son
they had shared no memories together
no photographs, no school plays, hobbies, or turkey days
no baseball tosses, no smiling faces, or consoling voices
to reassure him after nightmares and childhood losses
no pats on the back, no fishing trips
no ice for black eyes, or busted lips
no long walks, or heart felt talks

only feelings of emptiness
to hide away in secret places
and dreams of what could have been . . .
dreams of what should have been

seeing no commonality between them
except for supposed shared genes
she felt she should at least give him *"something"*
so, she decided to give him his father's pipe
she reached into a small brown paper bag
and revealed an old, worn-out pipe in her hands
it was decorated with imitation alligator hide
with teeth marks carved in the mouth piece

    "this was his favorite," she said

as she placed the pipe gently in his hands
as far as he knew, he didn't smoke
so, why the pipe? no one knows
why not an endowment, or some entitlement?
why not a photo of his likeness?
why not a watch? . . . a piece of jewelry? . . .
a family heirloom?
something that he could pass on to his son, and he to his

(Continued)

he felt its disappearing texture with his fingers
he put the pipe up to his nose
smelling the sweet aroma of mint flavored tobacco
he tried to conjure up an image
of what he must have been like
but he was unsuccessful
the pipe, and its aroma
only served as a reminder of things
un-said . . . things un-done . . .
things un-remembered . . .
this old worn-out pipe
with teeth marks carved in the mouth piece
was just another reminder
of one more thing
unshared